TO THE BARRICADES

STEPHEN COLLIS

D1363830

TALONBOOKS

© 2013 by Stephen Collis

Talonbooks
P.O. Box 2076
Vancouver, British Columbia, Canada V6B 3S3
www.talonbooks.com

Typeset in Meta and printed and bound in Canada
Printed on 100% post-consumer recycled paper

Cover: Carole Condé and Karl Beveridge, *Liberty Lost (G20, Toronto)*, 2010
© CARCC 2013
Cover design by Typesmith

First printing: 2013

The publisher gratefully acknowledges the financial support of the Canada Council for the Arts, the Government of Canada through the Canada Book Fund and the Province of British Columbia through the British Columbia Arts Council, and the Book Publishing Tax Credit for our publishing activities.

LIBRARY AND ARCHIVES CANADA CATALOGUING IN PUBLICATION

Collis, Stephen, 1965–
    To the barricades / Stephen Collis.
Poems.
Issued also in electronic format.
ISBN 978-0-88922-747-7
    I. Title.
PS8545.E22T6 2013   C811'.54   C2013-900154-9

reet barricades the barricade in the Rue a makeshift barricade built up into barricades dishor
rricade fluttered over the barricade a barricade had been started the barricades peep into
ades leapt down from the barricade re-entered the barricade the barricade with muskets sh
rricade the flag on the barricade climb onto the barricade building the barricade attack on
ade present within the barricades the whole dark barricade behind the barricade crashed
rricade stealthily towards the barricade other side of the barricade climbed onto the barric
up the barricade the barricade until the other end of the barricade anyone on the barrica
ade is nearly barricade which was constantly barricade and went the barricade and the v
rricade a sudden impulse where the barricade was situated the barricade may be taken
ade won't fall make them into a barricade on the barricade barricades most likely barric
normous this barricade alone barricade as though it were their hive barricades used everyt
arricade was mad barricade like a cliff observed the barricade barricades the discerna
ess the barricade within the barricade the barricade had devoured build the barricade
ade is sound barricades were gathering on this barricade this barricade of ideas the barric
tronger the barricade across the barricade across a barricade preparing a barricade no
r the whole barricade flashed fire facing the barricade would the barricade stand into
ade back to the barricade end of the barricade the barricade and the house the barricade w
along the barricade just outside the barricade the barricade into fire on the barricade in
ade attacking a street barricade to overthrow the barricade the barricade itself flung aga
rricade at the foot of the barricade defenders on the barricade factories as the barric
ding the barricade the barricade in the Rue barricades went up the barricade itself once
ade and over-run the barricade the barricade so long silent beyond the barricade not far f
rricade beyond the barricade the barricade scarcely peculiar to the barricade the barrica
eel emerging from the barricade the barricade always ships and barricades barricade for
se prepared the barricade gap in the barricade a street barricade on top of the barricade
rricade a rush for the barricade the small barricade saved the barricade from the top of
ade end of the barricade over the barricade the barricade formed over the barricade en
rricade assault upon the barricades every barricade why our barricade on the barricades
ade approached rushed the barricade flung upon the barricade the barricade under ass
rricade was subjected end of the barricade above the top of the barricade within the barric
shed in the barricade the barricade constructed compressing the barricade Titans
ade end of the barricade on top of the barricade in brief the barricade mended the barric
the barricade beyond the barricade to climb the barricade at the barricade guarded lo
ade here from the barricade the barricade muttered at the barricade at the barric
ted by the barricade on the barricade on the barricade to the barricade before me
ade at the barricade to the barricade the barricade unformed to the barricades to the barrica

street barricades the barricade in the Rue a makeshift barricade built up into barricades dish
barricade fluttered over the barricade a barricade had been started the barricades peep in
icades leapt down from the barricade re-entered the barricade the barricade with muskets
barricade the flag on the barricade climb onto the barricade building the barricade attack
icade present within the barricades the whole dark barricade behind the barricade crashe
barricade stealthily towards the barricade other side of the barricade climbed onto the bar
v up the barricade the barricade until the other end of the barricade anyone on the barric
icade is nearly barricade which was constantly barricade and went the barricade and the
barricade a sudden impulse where the barricade was situated the barricade may be take
icade won't fall make them into a barricade on the barricade barricades most likely bar
enormous this barricade alone barricade as though it were their hive barricades used ever
barricade was mad barricade like a cliff observed the barricade barricades the discer
ness the barricade within the barricade the barricade had devoured build the barricad
icade is sound barricades were gathering on this barricade this barricade of ideas the bar
stronger the barricade across the barricade across a barricade preparing a barricade
ger the whole barricade flashed fire facing the barricade would the barricade stand in
icade back to the barricade end of the barricade the barricade and the house the barricade
se along the barricade just outside the barricade the barricade into fire on the barricade
icade attacking a street barricade to overthrow the barricade the barricade itself flung a
barricade at the foot of the barricade defenders on the barricade factories as the bar
nding the barricade the barricade in the Rue barricades went up the barricade itself on
icade and over-run the barricade the barricade so long silent beyond the barricade not fa
barricade beyond the barricade the barricade scarcely peculiar to the barricade the barri
feel emerging from the barricade the barricade always ships and barricades barricade f
ose prepared the barricade gap in the barricade a street barricade on top of the barrica
barricade a rush for the barricade the small barricade saved the barricade from the top
icade end of the barricade over the barricade the barricade formed over the barricade
barricade assault upon the barricades every barricade why our barricade on the barricad
icade approached rushed the barricade flung upon the barricade the barricade under a
barricade was subjected end of the barricade above the top of the barricade within the bar
eshed in the barricade the barricade constructed compressing the barricade Titar
icade end of the barricade on top of the barricade in brief the barricade mended the bar
in the barricade beyond the barricade to climb the barricade at the barricade guarded
icade here from the barricade the barricade muttered at the barricade at the bar
ected by the barricade on the barricade on the barricade to the barricade before m
icade at the barricade to the barricade the barricade unformed to the barricades to the barri

The true drama of contemporary culture lies in the fact that it has become almost impossible to imagine social change that is not cataclysmic.
—Sven Lütticken

The poem distributes itself according to the necessity of subjects to begin, to begin speaking to anybody, simply because of the perception of continuous co-embodiment as the condition of language. This shaped speaking carries the breath of multiple temporalities into the present, not to protect or to sanctify the edifice of tradition, but to vulnerably figure historicity as an embodied stance, an address, the poem's most important gift to politics.
—Lisa Robertson

Dear Common

after Gerald Raunig's Art and Revolution

I had thought this was
Outside the barricades
No street in time
But a space left
Uneven and cluttered
With broken ballot boxes
Like a poem with
Everything in it so
Nothing you write
Isn't it and
Nothing you write is
But everywhere your
Hand over the page
Is shadowed by
Another hand taking
Up what you've written
Down and finding the
Spatiotemporal scale
At which it
Makes the most sense

It's not a matter of
Imposing no
Guidelines
So long as they—
Tinkering with the
Art machine / the
Revolutionary machine—
Rise up from below
Evading the narratives
Of major ruptures
1789 / 1917

And—constantly moving
Permeable fluctuating—
A swarm of points of
Resistance not crushed
By apparatus—they
Find their own way
To the supper of
All history's comers

I'm talking about a poem
And a revolution
Dear decaying discourse
The lacunae of every
Word we pitch
Brick by brick
Up against what
Contents and discontents
We are wanting
To wall out or
Wanting to wall in
One foot firm
In the reals
We have been
While the other
Steps off into the
Unimaginables we
Haven't

Or brushing the dust off
An old familiar form—
Say sweet fringe
Of what I think
I'm saying—I can
Feel your pulse
Wherever I touch
The hand you hold out
To my place within
Or without this poem

What's utterly common
What we set out
To accomplish together
Now that the entire world
Is one occupied square
Vibrating and red and
At the very edge of this page

Dear Common: Vancouver Alights

1. MILITANT PARTICULARISM

We are everywhere
in flight
annihilating space
one digital widget at a time
—is this what we
want it to be like?
Made a city
out of quotations
other voices
lived there too
I caught glimpses of them
in all the glass
where neon races
reflected the names
of bars and restaurants
that no longer exist
steering towards
uncertain markets
their boat in the street
a barricade we
could assemble ourselves

This was sort of
real / unreal
the city throbbing
gulped seajet years
primal terror
of spatial edges
where changeless
nothing pulses
against our fragile
real estate bubble

Thus we contrived power
electric sign illuminations
geographic billboard space
but that blast
of unevenness
snuffed our dwarfdom
left us rafts
a nude beach
glaring Hollywood
lights of Plutonian
descendants stretching night
to canvas crests
and gabled gateways
to imagined orients east

See the impact
on our bottom line
glows in the dark
lighting the dream world
of the collective
its lost halo
of sign culture
consuming sublime objects
like narrative it
threads us into
seductive structures one
neon tube at a time

Discordant vitality
will the soft porn
of windows allow
us to imagine
other Vancouvers
to alight on?
Cars race in reflection
everywhere red is
advertising itself a
young boy drives
a pretend shiv

into another's willing
abdomen—it's all
good fun—immigration
exclusion head taxes
house after house
confiscated for security's
racialized insecurity

Dear glittering ghost
to be watching
all this fading
around us—
that old fart's memories
this fence that once
formed a surface
for postering—
is to watch a
geographical transformation
(oiled by flowing
electronic accounts)
from mill-town glow
to metropolitan glare—
millwrights to lumpen extras
milling around the city set
of entertainments we
can no longer afford

Dear common crossing
Powell at night—
this is a love story
a recycled badge
used vacuum cleaner
punks outside the wig shop
shadows walking south—
the masters have no
mercy and the
Internet's growing arms
to pull us into
the soup of debt

Helpless puppets
magnetic ropes connect
earth's upper atmosphere
with the sun—
can't we give this
a good solid pull?
The body is porous
what is said seeps
into the skin
we absorb ideology
one camera click
at a time—
clerk waiter usher thief
the colony dismantled
its neon and shipped
out with the containers
crowding the pier
into the unlit "vacant"
space it erased—
boundary fixity surface
for a moment there
let us learn this
then put it in the pocket
of our endless open projects
engaging with closure
one backlit city block
at a time

2. THE FRICTION OF DISTANCE

If I could
smash you
found object if
I could collect debris
of defunct details
your order would
swoon under light
of fissures breed
music of similar
forms found wanting
shadows inverse lives
ethnic shadow shopping
shadow hip shadow
shadow in love shadow
on a cellphone gay shadow
looking to cross shadow
come silver come sunder
come light

Without resistance
brutal bond
without riot gear
tear gas dogs without
windows glass cars
overturned mailboxes broken
contents strewn smoke
without beatings and
without blood dear
common what have
we cameras for
fists and voices
consciences to say

oops I broke
arbitrary state /
corporate power
in rage of streets
torrents of bodies
without resistance just
the brutal bond

What if we washed
the streets away
drained the harbour of its
rusting ship water
and barricaded the parks
of all jogging
what if this was
the temper of temporality
and—spaced—we
vagranted our vision
to begin properly
unpropertied
what if linger was
a noun we held
in our hands carelessly
what if it whispered
what if it was
our only home

Ambulatory space of
cheap commodities
je t'adore
I want to walk unfettered
roadsides stroll past rivered
metal glint of light off
Toyotas and birds turning wing
signs of direction impossible
mileage to walk to press
feet past their folding
and the unfolding fields
to yield to movement many

microseconds of thoughtless
passage no refinement but
refineries along the river
opening out onto
uncertain tankered seas
something in the feet saying go
the cooked saying I
fought the raw and
the raw won

Go idiot wind
propel me beneath causeways
over concrete and canals
into the port
of impossible wealth
choked passages quoting money
Go time go space
squeeze me into the
light of these towers
lift bridges and tunnel
tunnels—we are over
and under all of this at once
Go body—you are
grease for the wheels
Go mind into information
buckets of data break
over your head—
this is the beginning
of endings or the end
of beginnings

Famine amidst abundance
callous cash payment
solid melts air
dear swept away
population conjured out
of the ground
melts solid air
block erased bricks

spatial fixes unfixed
sorcerers no longer
in control powers
leap into empty
urban wastes flowers
solid air melts
dear preserved facades of
commercial pasts pull
Tartarean tenderness down
into this liquid
market melts air
solid disquiet's accumulation
accumulates here

Kettle: Vancouver to Toronto [June 2010]

for Cecily Nicholson

this meagre
side-swipe of
telecommunications
each camera aimed
at each camera
capturing static
police state maimed
overthrow of actual
streets and actual
ideas rolling under
foot to hobble
not-quite round
spheres in our ears
and throngs at our backs

▢

tweet
after tweet
the sweet
hereafter
heaves
anger at
the devices
bringing us
this news
that flays
news but
leaves no
space for a
human response
dumb box
I kick

⬭

errant furies
in yellow reflective
vests mark
my words
these walls have
fears or its
tears welling

every staple and
pin ever driven
into this pole

every cop
that ever stopped
a kid with a
backpack and
brown skin

⬭

drip coffee on
keyboard
the feed
streams in new
video after new
video
ramping
discontent

meanwhile
over at the net
work cop
cars burn or
overturn as
reality runs
riot with
reporters'
calm demeanour

☐

soft
architects
form flexible
fencing round
ideological
limits—you
two-bit
skid don't
pony up to
this line
your song
no sonic
device
crowding
control
your longing
ski-masked
and pseudo we
pretend to
govern so
pretend to
move along

☐

fence apes
growth or
contributions to
knowledge
quicker way to
give pain the
corner target
cap oil well
its reconstituted
hospitals Haitian
season drowning in
numbers recovered
the gun when she

says constable
fires forests and
budget trampled feet

▭

movement is the
only movement is
resistance

bottled rain
crowd flow

the only resistance
to the thing
that keeps growing and
wait
shit moving too

and where can we
find the
lever or
switch which
turns this
fucking thing off?

▭

fighting for
fence to
prevent or
overcome
fence the

city indicted
will never be
united

and isn't
that the
kettle calling
the bloc black?

☐

a private
property slew
foot park
space sprayed
clubbed and
hoofed we

are biggest and
how do you think we
keep ourselves
biggest huh?
run you over and
truncheon for
delegates full of
CDN beef
slicked CDN oil
or jangled CDN gold

kettle a
bloc black
whose bloc
called the
kettle black
and what can
a poem do
for kettles calling
us back to
back our black blocs

☐

cold late distance
phone or net
its questions the
woods barrel through
how to link
all the changes
to no chain fences
when to be at the
table is to eat
what they serve?

each act police
states our anger
a trump card
batons our brains
we will accept
any measure will
we? it seems so
to sip from
proffered cups
we will fleece
constituent oils and
embargo everything toil
for a paltry or a naught

despair? it's just
the air at night
the fire and flames we
militantly report from
a camp called
hope just over
a few fences
from here
temporary detention
centre Canada or
whatever nations noose

Dear Common: Vancouver

I choose to believe in the natural consciousness,
I see what the deer see
—George Oppen

Dear common
in Vancouver we
slip amongst money
coast mists and
lumber memories
wondering if rain
falls equally upon
the heads of the
rich and poor
no noblesse for
this oblige as
companies mine death
to deliver largesse
but—city of
sightlines and sea
walls—where can I
lay my natural consciousness
here my animal spirits
unleashed into the
waters of the streams
corralled in culverts
beneath non-existent
paving stones?

Rhetoric is a glass
font a chromed
entrance to banks
and soaring offices
my language is
simple and inert

I might turn to
the sentence as a
prison or an escape
dire predictions stop
nothing the arteries
fill tunnels and
bridges with
unbarricaded traffic

A flash mob is
one thing the way
the mountains shoulder
their load of snows
is another
no Atlas no
Olympus but
to see what the
deer see is
a revolution of
another kind

▱

Dear apparatus of
accumulation you
platform for capital
we call home
there are demonstrations
and we demonstrate
police wear yellow
reflective vests and
some of us have
reflective vests too
directing traffic to
the manifestation
of other ends
no monetary reasons
in mind like I
could love another—

seems almost
ontological—the
lift of their
limbs or voice raised
no this no that
and affirmation
is the sound we make
individually though
somehow the same
spatially and temporally
united—you know
whose streets our
streets

⬚

Vancouver is not a
march or an
occupation but it
seems so in its
fixity where we'd
unleash all this
movement
course together
but work on
smoothing the edges
where one breaks off
and another begins

You see we
spilt this city
over indigenous land
mountain spirits down
to the midden
heaped beaches
something primitive
say commerce or
colonization the blunt
heads of culture

driving stakes until
indignant and damn
I kick my juice
if rhyme was a
drug I'd sell it
by the gram

Vancouver you
light between
mountains and a
sea where derricks crane
and condos never cease
to amaze

▢

Dear common a
city is no essence
but this conversation
this address is
something close
though it's tricky
to see clearly when
even the cops ride
bikes and green
things become a
market of seeming
values so boxed
voices say what
are you protesting
against the lap
of luxury and
medicinally planned
peace or is it just
your profession to be
in the street
all these signs and
bullhorns in your
basement just waiting

for a cause some
predictable riot against
government's disdain?

Dear effects of
tireless treason—
the social only
shuffles if you
move your feet
we've learned this
in a place invaders
called Vancouver
even if we are only
a few and even if
it rains on the day
of the demo

▢

Dear common what
we love about this
place is outside
the accumulation of
real estates or
pile-up of colonial
collisions on an
unmarked historical
highway bleeding resources
into chemical seas

You see—
as lights dimmed
over the DTES
and tents went up
in a vacant lot
where developers
dreamed of condos
sleek in their
reflective skins—

who could tell
just how far we were
from a nineteenth-century
Paris we built and
unwittingly rebuilt
in our radical minds?

I'll tell you
next time we stream
into the city
celebratory and decked
in red—it will be for
no hockey game
no civic or national
spectacle but the ghosts
of solidarities past
grabbing hold of
the material city
stone by
shaking stone to
heave it into
the sea or onto
a raven's sleek back

▭

If this weren't a poem
I would want to
talk of protests of
marches in these
streets the force of
voices and flags a
group singing loudly a
group carrying what
looks like a silk dragon a
group with masks and
a makeshift battering ram

I would want to
say Paris say
revolution say
Paris and Vancouver
touch known and
unknown but
it is not true
and we go on
ignorant of the we
we have been becoming
so long they say so long
to all that anger and
dissent so long
we are government and
you have nothing
to do with us
but we've everything
to do with you
so long Paris
hello Vancouver

Hold on hold
on I say I
ask have we
arrived yet have we
begun or even
returned from having
begun once before
hold on hold on
Brigette DePape
on the Senate floor
with your sign
stop Harper stop
Louis-Napoléon
we are coming
or we have been
or we are
on our way back
from a Paris in
our barricaded hearts

▭

Vancouver
I've seen you
on the day of a
protest stream along
streets to work
or between appointments
or yoga or shopping
in your various
hotnesses
ignoring us and the
noise we make
the colour of our
banners or the
precise words we've
printed there or which
we chant
the normal of banks
and starbucks and
boutiques oblivious
to the rain and the
gulls or pigeons hunched
above trolley wires

And I was frightened
by the grey stone
of your milled eyes
the crystal of
camera lenses
sound of a band
or game at the stadium
and I ran with
these strangled others
towards an endless
line of cops or
some large vacant
parking lot late
with nothing and

no one there
just a lone and
thin bear eating
garbage or an orca
gasping on the
pavement having
burst from the ground

July Days [1830]

It was easier to sing
In the smoke
Sell mementoes of
Unrequited consumption
Invertebrates we'd co-opted
And made into
A sort of fuel for
Our inconsolable bodies

Rewriting the regulations
Kept us busy
While the government of dolts
Blotted possibilities
New fashion statements
Made in chemical hues
Lingerie for your hybrid car

It was easier to sing
Prairie poets in their
Straight-line cavalcades
Than engage with the engines
Their spinning parts
All the ideology of
Powerlessness pooling under
New power lines

It was easier
And we took this
Chance to rest to
Recline in our poems
Our little art-shop lives
While the ground was
Eaten up and the air
Lit on fire and the
Water turned to dust

Dear Delacroix

Dear Delacroix what
sort of victory
was this regime's
costume change between
authoritarian acts you
witnessed from sidelines
your passion for
passion sending you
to covert canvas
when a vision comes up
girl in her glory
bright skin of Edens
fresh as formlessness
gun and flag
forming her Phrygian
capped liberty what
barricade this low
could have protected us
from the sameness
that settled in again?

Here I take the liberty
of quoting myself
Nature is a dictionary
imagination includes
the knowledge of all means
and the desire to acquire them
if one could draw
philosophical conclusions
from purely material phenomenon
ideas one thought
buried in the night
of the past
you explosion of lanterns
you fireworks of the
Goddess of liberty
brief as your enthusiasm
revolution's monument is
emptiness untold

Deputies dismissed and
the assembly dissolved
removed vestiges of freedom
fighting spread barricades
three glorious days overrunning
troops refusing to fire
and Ingres guarding the galleries
of the Louvre
while men whet the edges
of their weapons
on the paving stones
of the quays

An urchin brandishing
pistols a bourgeois
in top hat
an artisan with
a sabre a peasant
crawls half-dressed
body of a worker
two royal soldiers
small boy sporting
a stolen helmet
young student of
the École Polytechnique
missing shoes torn
and patched clothing
bits of military
bric-a-brac
spontaneous heroes
with bits of metal
in their broomsticks
sweeping the street

July is revolution
the sun in its
liberty cap and
red flag three glorious
days unfolding regimes
ruin a kind of
wingless victory the
very subject proletarian
no risk of her cap
being confused with a crown
projection of the real
and the unreal
enlarged reality not
pallid academic allegory
after image of
July revolutions history
in the guise of art
her breasts to feed
future's musculature

Hasty relegation
of his *Barricades* to
the cellars of the Louvre
but July's revolution
paid the companion
piece did not appear
in 1848 or did it
in Meissonier's heap
of broken bodies
or Thibault's daguerreotype
of the rue Saint-Maur
no lady leading
no people not
in the azure sky
nor on this poor earth
where perfection itself
is imperfect and
patriarchs arch their
backs in allegorical femininity

Dear heap of bricks
I died for
Line I held
a lantern over
so others might
find the way
to stony resistance
barricade I guard
through dreams of
centuries to come
where liberty makes
a work of art
out of odious
subjects I
have not laid
to rest the
person of other
days nor her
hopes and dreams
of the future
I am your etc.
your continuation mounts
what cap she now
sports I cannot
name the logos of

Dear Common: Study for the rue Saint-Maur [1848]

> *Walls built without attention given to levelling,*
> *drainage and binding often disintegrate as a result*
> *of winter's freezing and thawing.*
> —Curtis Fields, *The Forgotten Art of Building a Stone Wall*

The ends of pipes drip
Emotion or write
Cities back to
Jumbled origins as
In unfenced space
People gravitate
Towards margins
While in fenced
Space they spread out
Evenly (unevenly)
And found cities
And countries and
Economies so let us
All loose against
Limits dreaming beyond
All striving to come
Into existence where
There is a buried
Quotation from Paul Celan

Dear common this
Has become personal
For all of us
Our species beings
Torn by heat
And profit in each
And every instance
There must be a speaking
And an acting out

And against these
Blinders as guardrails
The fires in oil skies
The chemical wind
And the banks
And the nations
And the pretend greenery
Surrounding money

Stop this day
And night with me
Digging a grave in the sky
Or raise a lament
As together we're thrown
Against this Facebook
Mur des Fédérés this
Global moment's big tent
Falling around our heads
Spiralling videos
As we destroy the very
Terms of our slippery
Existence and photograph
The barricades from
Above for our inner
Cavaignacs
And the rue Saint-Maur
Looks quiet
In the pre-dawn
As poetry assumes its
Stillness once again

La Commune [1871]

1.

In the spring of 1871
In June 1848
On September 4 1870
As was the case in 1830 and 1848
Early on the morning of 18 March
Between 21 May and 28 May
Between March and May 1871
During the Cultural Revolution
Outside the revolution of 17 October
The Parisian workers of 18 March 1871
When Lenin danced in the snow
Over the terrible days of June 1848
The *Trois Glorieuses* of July 1830
February 1848 and the fall of Louis Philippe
As regards 1830, 1848, and 1870
On the evening of the resistance in the workers' districts
The declaration of 19 March 1871
Since at least 1830
Again in May 1968
In the uncertain world of the spring of 1871
From 18 March to May 28 1871, the brute force of uprisings
This beginning called 18 March
18 March, now a predicate
Under the sign of an eruption of being
By which "18 March" comes to appear
The site a figure of the instant
Will dictate to them the morning of 19 March
This empirical 18 March
A consequence of 18 March
The enthusiasm of 18 March 1871
When on 10 May the central committee proclaimed
Whose result is that "18 March" gets instituted

To save the revolution of 18 March
In all certainty on 18 March 1871
By October 1917
By the summer of 1967 in China and May 1968 in France
Let's return to 19 March
Three times the French proletariat made the republic for others
On 18 March something more important was destroyed
Whatever therefore its fate at Paris
Beginnings can then be measured by the re-beginnings they authorize
The task is to think its content

2.

Revolution
is the search for happiness

we know history
repeats itself

thanks
to all the dead anarchists!

I make you a chain of flowers
a grave of roses

now let's not lack audacity
in dealing with the banks

even in a democracy
we aren't free to demonstrate   freely

things kept germinating
long after the event

it's time we stop being
represented and start   being

the commune echoes
we're still at the same point

▢

Same ideas
other methods

to get out of this shit
burn down markets

shout out
of streets

whose streets?
our streets

but we fell asleep
at some point

the film went on
another world was

not yet possible
today we need more

than a barricade
the street is wired

maybe a wall
in time too hmm?

▢

When it's up
to each person

to be their
own barricade

then we've lost
thrown ourselves

down solitary wells
where capital wants us

where is the enemy now
what wall in what street

can keep them out
or keep us safe?

we are all the commune
they want to kill

with sleepy devices
apps and gigs

is this poem
too easily read?

is it doing anything
to end oppression?

we're searchable yes
but we can still search too

the cops use barricades now
when did we give them up?

the question is: are we
going to rest   or wrest?

3.

We common
Parisian into our texts
pry books up and
make a heap across
the read street

We've had our labour
dematerialized
we shatter data and
stack up bits

We common
have our entertainments too
the business of
scores and scales
operates the pleasure
of our insides
soothing our least
and our levers

We have an angry
indignant threat too
we keep for
public shouting:
it coughs trying
not to disturb us
in some night
folded in our city

Common
will culture
keep us safe
or just sell us
to the highest bidder?

Common don't
tell them we're
open don't
tell them our hearts
have sleeves
the shelter we've
made in this structure
is a surplus mostly unseen

Dear common
I think we should
up the anti
get even more
against it turning
all tables all
cobblestones all streets

Or—and I know
this is exactly the
opposite of that—
admit we know nothing
about art or revolution
or the glint of light
on damp utopian streets

Get out of the way
stop making so much
noise and quietly
listen to our vowels
and the way they
come up against
consonants the gaps
between words
between paving stones
between people

Commune
we have not failed
though we have been
shot against the
walls of May
(where later
it was easier
to meet us with
tear gas clubs
pepper spray
mass media disdain
feed us soda pop
and video games
trampled into the
dust of disregard
while amped-up
powers managed to
hide themselves
in discourse paring
their fingernails
to one side of money)

Or if we have failed
this failure is the
maintenance of
continuing possibility
if only we remember
that we once tried
that we can try again
and that this is
what strikes fear
into the industry
of false hopes and
mindless entertainments

Commune
they have us all
on the wrong side
of the global tracks
watching the show
unfold on the other
1871 through 2011

Commune
which side will
you be on?
Can you see
what is happening
as the puppets drop
from the hands of
hidden dictators
reaching for their
balance sheets
guns and cameras?

Commune
does it make sense
to speak this way
anymore? The terms
"us" and "them"
are being re-inscribed
each day to
"their" advantage—
where is it that "we"
fell off the map?
Absence is contagious
just ask every
revolutionary nobody
we have long forgotten

But if we could
find that place
we went invisible
maybe some
shooting gallery in
an eternal Paris
side of a cable
TV truck or city
intersection once
blocked by barricades
we might through
the magic of
atemporal solidarity
conjure ourselves back
onto the brink
arm raised with a stone—
everywhere some kid
with a stone in front
of soldiers and tanks

Commune
I like a little
crack in my
sidewalks a
gap between
my cobbles—your
monuments to
barbarism—how
are they built now?
All glass
aren't they—
see that stone
lying there
Commune?
See your
reflection in that
bank or department
store window?
How many hands
do you have
Commune?
How many years
of bad luck
have you already
suffered smashing
nothing?

Commune
I'm writing this
after the fact

In Egypt in 2011
bumper stickers proclaim
"today I won't run
traffic lights
I will change"

Something is
happening Commune
and we are it
but the question is
will we be different
than the last time
as farce is
to tragedy was?

Commune I hope so
listening to the words
of Ahmed Fouad Negm
echoing across Tahrir

Commune
we are an endless poem
and we are right here
at your elbow

4.

In the middle of October 2011
When in September 2011
Then in October in cities across
While October was brewing
On January 25 2011
Because of May 15 2011
Because the Indignados had already been
That was in January 2011
September 17 2011 it began with
No one was much aware before September 24 when
Nearly one thousand cities on October 15
The movement of May 15 had
City squares on October 15 when
January 2011 will be remembered for
Global day of action on October 15 2011 as
When we heard about the May 15 movement
Inspired by the events of January and February in Egypt
No one could have guessed on January 25 that
But without May 15 2011
On September 17 in Lower Manhattan just
Occupy Everywhere October 15 2011
Wall Street on September 17 2011 was where
Towards the Puerta del Sol on the eve of May 15
Not even the Egyptians on February 2 2011 could have
Our Martyrs of January and February 2011 never had
In the surprising Spring of 2011
As the long Spring of 2011 began to
Then in the fall of 2011
After the September 24 video went viral
Long after October 15 although we still are not

To the Barricade on rue de Tourtille [May 28, 1871]

> *The completion of each section provides contrast*
> *between the new and the old and gives further*
> *incentive to dismantle and rebuild the next section.*
> —Curtis Fields, *The Forgotten Art of Building a Stone Wall*

In the fields
Lightning flashes
Where until now
Only madness reigned
And every city
Is beautiful to me
Despite the tidal wave
Of conservatism
Uneven development
And global gunplay

Though the scope may
Have become smaller
The walls against which
We are shot have
Grown wider and
The means of "shooting"
More varied / finessed
Televised and updated
The reform of consciousness—
The dream about ourselves—
That much harder to
Awake from the coffins
We carry mobile in our hands

But I digress
The differentials
Of time hold secrets
We can't unlock—

Dear final foray
Last barricade
Of the commune—bees
Lift subway tiles and
Lakes leave gated beaches—
It is forever nearly dawn
A small animal still
Escapes a battered downspout
Children continue to mould
Lead bullets with thimbles
While at night girls once
Again drag paving stones
To the barricades
Where they've occupied
The city centres
Some sort of tool
At work on their hearts
Tinkering away
At the battle for tomorrow

RELUMINATIONS 1

Barricades involve a kind of bricolage, a
provisional cobbling together of whatever bits
and pieces come usefully to hand ... this may
also serve as a perceptive account of the poetic
techniques of a Rimbaud, indeed of the
revolutionary avant-garde in general.
—Fredric Jameson

Amidst trembling
dirty streets
a piano
the tangled heap
of spring
waters & sorrows
since subsided
dear bodies
rustling treetops / islands
this song stops
clocks that don't strike

Murmur
of the end of the world
I feel fine
the tomb illuminates
nothing
maybe gulfs
seas & fables / silence

▢

Revolution
come up with something better
broad human gardens
torched palaces

the crowds
ecstatic amidst destruction
the promise of love
missing from our desire
dementias tricks perform
they transform people
tears & terror

a savage sideshow

Cities of noise & affection
shouting in the public square
the new harmony:
change
the substance of always

I remember rivers
the masterpieces of chaos
polemics

I don't miss the air

Transformed
I am waiting to become
peculiar or just
inventive

☐

Once memories smother you
throw your
impossible voice
as public funds
into the clouds

O February
our poverty
stirred up

smoke & looms
O other world
dragging behind us
spent in its chrome fixtures

The banks can jacket instruments
fragments of publics / fail

▭

Every monument
reduced
I see spectres
of the wood
death without
crime
life without
election

Cities collapse
humming crops fail
our weapons braying
ideas of the people
new work / movements

To find the location
& the recipe
of our invented explosion

▭

Age of poverty
the market illuminated
at the bottom of the river
& the beloved world
was only blueprints
of logical accidents
groups with creatures

& carpets
the sound of waves
halfway up the walls

The compost
of progress
creates the blue
abyss

Brambles swirl
towards the light

& skyrockets meander
with romantic indigents

▭

After beings
live coals raining down
the terrestrial refugees
wheeling
O world
boiling to the depths
& orchestral energies
forget all limitations
anarchy for the people
& the future

Dying choir
glass collapses
but harmonic &
architectural possibilities
rouse the world
& will become
nothing like today

As revolts swarm Empire
& a little world
is constructed

& impossible boats deposit us
on angry planets where
the extermination of every being
will not be permitted

☐

Since reality
I found my wing
the fields
the suburbs throw

The door is open
to human misery
other beings
disincorporated
& the banks
the world's conquerors
seeking chemical fortunes

Enlightened by the machinery
themselves meteorological accidents

☐

City centers
nourish rebellions
monstrous industrial or
military exploitation

Farewell
we'll adopt
ferocious philosophies
shambling world
this is the real

Amidst rage & troubles
we reinvent the future
now its promise resounds:
this age has sunk!

Now forms & action
lift suffering life
O world!
the crowd / our strength & feelings
seeing / breathing / body / day

RELUMINATIONS 2

> *It is ... not necessary for these barricades to be*
> *perfectly constructed; they can very well be made*
> *of overturned carriages, doors torn off their hinges,*
> *furniture thrown out of windows, cobblestones*
> *where these are available, beams, barrels, etc.*
> —Cluseret

the streets have felt much of the century

arch of sky   all art and activity

that there are breadlines

quotations like robbers

who leap out armed

who aim to not only have the most

who encased in the core of a shell

who loved their metonymic body parts

who help me understand all those love songs and how
the artists must have felt when writing them

▢

I feel I say a drink might help

for sale unheard of animals

towers fired upon simultaneously

future prospects smaller than today

after the feast of flying bricks

we recommend a midnight train

a Garry oak on southern Vancouver Island.

▢

the beginning of the impossible is here or nearby

its phantom limbs and silver flanges

the goods the mob captures coats

a collection of obsessions, oblique references, and footnotes

keep munching until all the animal is gone

▢

I am part Neanderthal, genetics confirms

the difference is when someone runs out of money

cuts descending on brokers in a trading room

burning car after burning car

become a regular form of expression for the disenfranchised

occupied or indignant or just plain appalled

▢

the storm of the future grows skyward

inanimate but reaching down into the orchestra pit

hedgies with a philanthropic bent

the politicians were for sale this whole time?

randomly rising inside the auditorium

get ready to jump into the abyss

that consumer society attaches so much value to

☐

somehow expected radicals and activists to be falling
out of every doorway

do they not know the flood has come and gone?

burp once for yes, twice for no

nooks of the ruined bank (formerly a starbucks)

keep munching until all the animal is gone

☐

on the chaotic untitled works of cities

avant-garde memories of the Good Old Days

the economy will have to muddle

into a police state youth have rejected

as we swing back and forth between moments of clarity

and densities we cannot explain

☐

this was a bank now it's a starbucks

to deal with the crushing debt

a forest full of beautiful trees

I must confess to a little pessimism about the future

give me online shelter

gather round an overturned bus

real crowd-pleaser

then grant some of them a rage effect / some of them agency

▢

Prospero's phone books

bad faith seizures by police

designed for generations at the end of the alphabet, *aight*?

disruptively Better Business

now blizzard decides to screw us here in cataclysm

cue voice-over of slow-drawling veteran talking about

heiress / media whore he very soul of this establishment

▢

what a week it has been in climate change!

there's not much meat on these bones—a stew?

they didn't really need the police after all, huh.

gilded wooden animals, tiny fish, seraphic centauresses

it's not as much like *Withnail and I* as I'd expected

you can't eat money *or* poems

▢

disjunction, I lay you across my knees and spank your reddening bottom

merchant of blemish

it was a landslide—except that, you know, not that many people voted

that gum you like is going to come back into style

you know that thing we keep doing that we keep calling "liberation"?

I have a haz-mat suit and a rag soaked in vinegar

▢

artist that blankness cannot actually mirror

find a lyric hole to curl up in

today, it does not matter

what is it like to have albinism?

I feel I say a drink might help

back to mermaids back to dredging

RELUMINATIONS 3

> *Poetry will no longer give rhythm to action;*
> *it will be in advance of action*
> —Rimbaud

Out in those hills
the avant-garde is on patrol

at a sandbar

two ducks discuss the Haitian revolution

things go on
investments mergers acquisitions

lawns being cut
by bankers on holiday

thinking of the death
of every blade

I drew what the
words were reciting

visions of boats
crossing dry land

helicopters lingering over
vacant corporate towers

Each animal had
some response to the flood

We whirled about in the
density of traumas

There wasn't enough
medicine for the fish

An opiate outlasts
a civilization

You can see its residue
in images on cavern walls

An apocalypse is
not that
distressing

Each animal
carries its extinction
in its code

I've come upon
prairies and
rivers

Not once did they
seem to be
the same

Each moment
the story goes
is flitting by

What's distressing is
the end of
potentiality

Even these
hypothetical erasures
would no longer exist

The idea that
exceeds matter
exceeding no more

I became a naturalist
once there was no more nature

Social cues missed by oblivious voters
everyone moving farther from the sea

The pages of every book faded to blank
someone opened a shop selling trinkets

precious metals that once
powered social networks

The only customers had
fur and feathers

I drew each one as it
loped off with its purchase

To line the nests of bowerbirds
and build barricades on the reef

A river rinses through
everything I think
poems animals haven't written
occupations   austerity measures

Some of us are funny
dolphins dead in drift nets
laugh at extinct tuna
it's not as bad as it seems

Small birds take up data mining
they are drawn to the word "tweet"
springboks march on Johannesburg
red flags flutter from their horns

Waterfowl in a brake
gather to mark the anniversary
of the Paris Commune
though not many of them are fluent in French

Who hasn't gushed at presentations?

A reading is given for grizzlies
feasting on dead salmon
seems like a sustainable economy
though no one has asked the salmon

Nothing is and nothing isn't language
releasing pheromones is not the same
as a constitution
though voles get along without representation

We are not drunk on italics
at a sidebar lawyers mewl in heat
a wolf says it owns this font and
eels download questionable content

Extinction is just the inverse
of rebellion
one by one they are boycotting being
it's better to be archived as fossils

for robots to find in some future
or so we might be led to assume
coming up with aliens as
we run out of animals

The outcome of events is uncertain
these linen things needing
this yarn needing animal coats

I have a feeling of
elderly people taking down governments

and we slip outside the market
and some are still casting their votes
and your hand is a water
I slip my animal hand into

your hair invisible black coats
your scent falling through my fingers

To the outer edge of
economies and ecologies
a pouch in which we meet
a subtle space the flood won't fill

Barricades Mystérieuses

1.

I don't know
What wind brought it here
To douse candles
Found in other people's poetics
Like references to
Figures from pop culture
That make us laugh a little
Because they are awkward
And embarrassed to be seen
In the baroque parlour
Of some sleepy
Pseudo-commodity of a poem
Or so we are told and expect

But it was here
Just the same—
Crescendo of Radiohead's
"Karma Police"—the
Felt presence of my
Dead sister
Wordsworth-like
Handing me the text
Of the perfect revolutionary poem
Which does not exist

This was my literal stage
A lyric brilliance
You couldn't escape
I stepped out back to smoke
Which I don't do—
The sky was just like the sky
A car in reverse might

Speed sloppily away from
And that wind was still
Blowing
The fire was spreading
New notes of another music
And I knew I didn't want
To write poems like that
Anymore

2.

In *Dr. Strangelove*
There's that colonel
Thought it was the water
Started shooting up his office
And Peter Sellers
Playing more than one character
Did not ride a bomb
Down over Russia
Or through a Texas night
Hot with executions

I tear down and rebuild
The book a hundred times
In some badly lit garage—
It doesn't matter
Art will always fail us
Our radical friends
Accidentally saying
"Trotskyite organist"
Choose refusal one
After another an
Opaque sky will open
And barricades will only appear
In streets I've never
Walked or driven down

I cough into the puppet
On my hand
It's face contorted behind
Dark sunglasses
A professor of only
Pretend politics

Peter Sellers pulls his arm
Back down into his wheelchair
Struggling to control
A gesture we recognize
For a minute there
With an uncomfortable laugh

Poetics against the Enclosure of Dissent

I want to become
Blunt
Stone axe or hammer
Word hit square on its
Referential head
To refute all arrayed
Against biome and being

But
Zipline Olympics
Rout of catatonics snapping pics
Peace sign photos in front of
Riot cops then
Video games what?

While these *enemies* I want to say
Artifice and stance
Proclaim riots to be
Without (dis)contents
Rioters
Without reasons
Looting hoods
One size fits all
Jumpsuit and jail

Thugs, they won't listen
As protest burns its definition
And nothing's too legit
That they won't quit
The locks and padlocks forming

Dear Common: Occupy

1. TO THE OCCUPATIONS

What half-light
goes collateral
seams of the
tents and tarps
of being lit
just dull
morning red
and blue
music almost
audible cars
wet streets and
we are mud
for forming
shapes plastic
which is to say
bending not
breaking
a bite to
place quickly
on cops' sleeves

To the
occupations
because we have
ideologically
confined spaces
Internet lies shot
not irons
fires—the
infrastructure
tent food
not bombs
tent media
tent tomorrow
tent tent
we will build
to the stars
and horizons
together

To the
occupations
because
they will helmet
baton and
legislate
the length of
this land in
media blackout
the silent sweeping
jail street jive
grabbing
girls by their
hair or just
clubbing the
aging protestor
as he rants and rails

To the
occupations
not for lack of
other employment
only the titled
see entitlement
and idiots
will ninjas to
appear in their
minds and
would rather
the easy hate
of each other
than the machinery
of state and money
eating them alive

To the
occupations
because they
are our barricades
now and
we will not
forget the
ransom for
profit each
debt an earth
occupied already
for centuries
at social and
ecological thresholds
we're waking
in our tents
to shake the ground
of mornings

2. BETWEEN SYMPTOM AND CRITIQUE

for Rob Budde

You have to
measure it with
your hands
the velocity
of the existing
emancipating
death wishes or
protesters their
police escort
just going out
of sight to
triangulate
photo finishes
like oil tankers or
polyjuice potion
drunk by executives
transformed
into "citizens"

Or the muddle
gone impossible
landscapes
buffer of air
bags myth
where animals
are skinned
after breaking
the windshield
of ideology

That is a
cut glass
or thrown across
the telescope
the premise is
can we jack
knife or
economic
pearl an
oyster
clandestine
and evading
the murk of
pipelines to
Kitimat these
oily fossils these
hulls

Orthodox
physics the
devil's club
won't let
the riff
won't chorus
unction or
ounce who
weighs kilos
anyway
the tar sands
insist
tomorrow's
just crud
left in our
contraptions

So hey you
protest kids
velvet these
undergrounds or
moths crazy
like bitumen
rivers
where a
language has
no word for
the habit of
candles
occupied
squares
ontological
in the nets of
love

3. HASHTAG INFINITY

Then they
broke camp
went for
orthography
of cardboard signs
to run banks
not bulls so
our insurgency
is livestreamed
a pop song over
tear gas streets
and cops their
chaperone eyes
seeing only a
percent etched
into paycheque
and all the
drills of empty
diversion

Leitmotif is
human microphone
all shouts will
be repeated
just don't yell
"fire" yell "bailout"
the bucket will
list the ship
run aground the
tankers yawl in
our harbours of
discontent and
Wall Street won't
bubble it'll
drown a rat
that got off
at the last port

Not just liberal
like Hedges the
field-to-fold ratio
or barricades
taken back from
Spartan cops
who appropriated
radical form their
plastic shields
reflecting the
communist horizon
of forgotten futures
we're remembering
now as kids in masks
throw tents all over
our consciousness

So stumbling
out of tempest
to clamber each
street we
demand
futures not just
pasts but
real rents
in the fabric
of the real
we demand
possibility
Lefebvrean
explosions
not just
Žižek spitting
in the park
but the future's
ruins lying all
about us waiting
to be pried up
from the ground
as we *toma la
calle* again

Tired old
proletariat now
googled into being
Marx would have
Luxemburg Che
Durruti Marcos
or any other
thrown red ink
and more
at this crisis so
we demand difference
demand alter
and anew
the cobblestones
and the fields
we demand
this continue
some shape or form
until we are all outside
money and mechanism
on a common
that's waiting to download

Come the Revolution

for Larissa Lai

1.

Come the revolution
we will the revolution
we will return to the
revolution return to the
sensuous body of language
come the revolution
we will return to the
sensuous body and
sound will propel us
through the barricades
of others the revolution
through the barricades
of otherness and come
as mere sparks will
spark us come
the revolution anew
and we will the
revolution come anew
and irony will no longer
bind us the sensuous
body of language lift us
fringe to feather to fold us
the sensuous body of
our methods
singletogetherness and
come the revolution
we will have time
the revolutionary time
to live the silent lives

of animals the revolution
animals we have lost
that is animals we have
killed the extinctions
corrupt economies come
the revolution throwing
throwing off sparks and
new economies and throwing
sound will propel us through
the revolution sensuous
the animal walls we are
as producers and consumers
as time and sound and
the sensuous body of language
will come the revolution when
banks will have shaken
banks shaken to shivers
shivers come the revolution
all fossils fuel for their
own revolution will come
and walking as sound
through sensuous bodies
formed we will walk
through an endless park
sensuous a park we will
walk from each of our abilities
to each of our needs
through sound the revolution
come sensuous come stroll
come the revolution we will
roll through birdsong and
singular birches come
the transformations of home
and together the revolution
this ecos will echo the
sensuous body I speak of
together the revolution
through this other's
effulgence so others

come the revolution
we will echo new limits we will
wrap self-governance in limits
wrap the sensuous body
of human tongue in animal revolution
self-governance in bios in animal
wrap sound all lifted to be level
to small habitations and
habits to be level
animal and sound and sensuous bodies
small hearths of animals own
all of us all animals
come the revolution we will
come to be animal to be sound
sing the revolution we will
sing the swords out of songs
sing swords into songs
songs through flowers through fields
sing bees through these fields
sing chemicals out of oceans
sing economies capacities even
sing balance sing home sustainable
sing sustainable come sound
sensuous bodies sustainable
sing songs of the absence
of oil and death in the oceans
          unsustainable
of tanks and guns and air strikes
          unsustainable
of endless colonial occupations
          unsustainable
profit motive and equity investments
          unsustainable
sing come the revolution
sing a jubilee for all the revolution
sing come hammer come storm
the revolution will come and we will
as animals as sensuous bodies
begin to be born

2.

Here is hoping
against all the investments
hedged against hope

Here is the past
in ruins all around us
its garden ideology gnomes
liberty caps and barricade stones

Here we are picking
up the pieces to hurl
to heal to build another world
still compound with catastrophe
and urging the revolution to come

Here we are still doubting
all apparatus of our
demobilization machines inching still
towards the cusp of no movement

⬭

Here is a feeling
for another structure
a class pokes its head up
says you are one of us
at least most of you are
maybe or do so now and again

Survivors of the elements
capital has composed
and decomposed

as a storm where
there is no climate
of change

☐

Here we come upon a problem:
what if our rebellion
has been congruent
with the gradual transition
to this more flexible capitalism?

I put a pup tent
on the palatial corporate lawn
the long global slump
yawns at our lack of a political project

Here we reside near the notion
of the new and better version
anything point 0
ripping its interface
off in the wind

Here we go back to the street
as we would back to a drawing board

But what if they ban chalk?
what if the pavement has no
stones we can pry up
our masks the illegal
look of anything states decline?

☐

Here we are still
in the ruins of crumbling system
or soon will be
keystone cop species
dressing our wounds
in the silk of forgotten luxury

A riot's a riot
unless you've no other choice
biting down
in order to get back up

did we mention the birds
nesting in the corporate edifice?

Here I'd gently whisper
"fuck the state
long and hard"

Biting the hand that feeds
because it feeds us just enough
to shut the factory when it chooses
and close the future before it arrives

3.

Come the revolution
poetry will make something happen
a machine that kills fascists
coiled at the core of a problem
the solution for which
is only conceivable in these terms

Come the revolution
I will no longer need
the oppressor's language
to speak to you
and the map of our failures
will have led to this victory
a house holding fracture and a loom
with nothing between us
we will no longer be broken

Come the revolution
I will lift a voice of everyone
and in the poem everyone
will be listening and I will say we are
free or a force and we will be
saying this and we will be
free and we will be a force and
I will say we are broken but whole
and equally so and we will
all be broken but whole and equally so and
I will say I am with you and we are
rising and I will say this in the form
of a poem and we will be
saying this and we will be together and we will be
rising in the tireless forms of our poems

Come the revolution
culture flourishes not in isolation
but enriched by the simple connection
of our belonging to the
belonging to the land so that
everywhere we are the animals
that know too well we are the animals
that must find our limits and love them
and we will govern ourselves within them
seeking agreement before confrontation
without government a political class
or the media that accompanies them

Come the revolution
shit will no longer be
fucked up and bullshit
and that which is loving in our hands
will touch that which is loving
in each and every other's hands
and while reading this poem still won't be the same
as storming a bank or a parliament
you may yet be reading this poem
to a group of people with whom you will presently
be storming a bank or a parliament

eet barricades the barricade in the Rue a makeshift barricade built up into barricades dishor

ricade fluttered over the barricade a barricade had been started the barricades peep into

des leapt down from the barricade re-entered the barricade the barricade with muskets sh

ricade the flag on the barricade climb onto the barricade building the barricade attack on

de present within the barricades the whole dark barricade behind the barricade crashed

ricade stealthily towards the barricade other side of the barricade climbed onto the barric

p the barricade the barricade until the other end of the barricade anyone on the barrica

de is nearly barricade which was constantly barricade and went the barricade and the v

ricade a sudden impulse where the barricade was situated the barricade may be taken

de won't fall make them into a barricade on the barricade barricades most likely barric

ormous this barricade alone barricade as though it were their hive barricades used everyth

rricade was mad barricade like a cliff observed the barricade barricades the discern

ss the barricade within the barricade the barricade had devoured build the barricade

de is sound barricades were gathering on this barricade this barricade of ideas the barric

ronger the barricade across the barricade across a barricade preparing a barricade no

the whole barricade flashed fire facing the barricade would the barricade stand into

de back to the barricade end of the barricade the barricade and the house the barricade we

along the barricade just outside the barricade the barricade into fire on the barricade in

de attacking a street barricade to overthrow the barricade the barricade itself flung aga

rricade at the foot of the barricade defenders on the barricade factories as the barric

ing the barricade the barricade in the Rue barricades went up the barricade itself once

de and over-run the barricade the barricade so long silent beyond the barricade not far f

ricade beyond the barricade the barricade scarcely peculiar to the barricade the barric

el emerging from the barricade the barricade always ships and barricades barricade for

e prepared the barricade gap in the barricade a street barricade on top of the barricad

rricade a rush for the barricade the small barricade saved the barricade from the top o

de end of the barricade over the barricade the barricade formed over the barricade en

ricade assault upon the barricades every barricade why our barricade on the barricades

de approached rushed the barricade flung upon the barricade the barricade under ass

ricade was subjected end of the barricade above the top of the barricade within the barri

hed in the barricade the barricade constructed compressing the barricade Titans

de end of the barricade on top of the barricade in brief the barricade mended the barri

the barricade beyond the barricade to climb the barricade at the barricade guarded l

ade here from the barricade the barricade muttered at the barricade at the barri

ted by the barricade on the barricade on the barricade to the barricade before me

de at the barricade to the barricade the barricade unformed to the barricades to the barric

street barricades the barricade in the Rue a makeshift barricade built up into barricades dis
barricade fluttered over the barricade a barricade had been started the barricades peep i
icades leapt down from the barricade re-entered the barricade the barricade with muskets
barricade the flag on the barricade climb onto the barricade building the barricade attack
icade present within the barricades the whole dark barricade behind the barricade crash
barricade stealthily towards the barricade other side of the barricade climbed onto the ba
w up the barricade the barricade until the other end of the barricade anyone on the barri
icade is nearly barricade which was constantly barricade and went the barricade and the
barricade a sudden impulse where the barricade was situated the barricade may be tak
icade won't fall make them into a barricade on the barricade barricades most likely ba
enormous this barricade alone barricade as though it were their hive barricades used eve
barricade was mad barricade like a cliff observed the barricade barricades the disce
kness the barricade within the barricade the barricade had devoured build the barrica
icade is sound barricades were gathering on this barricade this barricade of ideas the ba
stronger the barricade across the barricade across a barricade preparing a barricade
ger the whole barricade flashed fire facing the barricade would the barricade stand in
icade back to the barricade end of the barricade the barricade and the house the barricade
se along the barricade just outside the barricade the barricade into fire on the barricade
icade attacking a street barricade to overthrow the barricade the barricade itself flung a
barricade at the foot of the barricade defenders on the barricade factories as the bar
nding the barricade the barricade in the Rue barricades went up the barricade itself on
icade and over-run the barricade the barricade so long silent beyond the barricade not fa
barricade beyond the barricade the barricade scarcely peculiar to the barricade the barr
feel emerging from the barricade the barricade always ships and barricades barricade
ose prepared the barricade gap in the barricade a street barricade on top of the barrica
barricade a rush for the barricade the small barricade saved the barricade from the top
icade end of the barricade over the barricade the barricade formed over the barricade
barricade assault upon the barricades every barricade why our barricade on the barricad
icade approached rushed the barricade flung upon the barricade the barricade under a
barricade was subjected end of the barricade above the top of the barricade within the bar
eshed in the barricade the barricade constructed compressing the barricade Tita
icade end of the barricade on top of the barricade in brief the barricade mended the bar
in the barricade beyond the barricade to climb the barricade at the barricade guarded
icade here from the barricade the barricade muttered at the barricade at the bar
ected by the barricade on the barricade on the barricade to the barricade before n
cade at the barricade to the barricade the barricade unformed to the barricades to the barr

Dear Common: "Politics Is Its Own World, Whose Actors Have Probably Never Heard of 'The Idea of Order at Key West'"

after Ramon Fernandez

1.

But has the "Idea
of Order at Key West"
heard of the actors
slipping in and out of character
in the world of politics?
One there sings
beyond the genius
of the sea
a species of speech
that no longer has
the equipment to respond
to a general audience—
but this dying discourse
is still ours—
even in politics' own world
we are the makers
of our songs amongst
the meaningless plungings
aesthetics demands
will to change
power to speak
through and *between* the words
that lurch in a sentence—
that blind spot just beyond
the last strand of punctuation
wondering why it is
I constantly write poems
in which the actors vote
on the necessity of their worlds

2.

We could perhaps imagine
better communicative equipment
something that takes molecules
instead of words
from one being to another
implanting the material sense
of the sender in the receiver
launching new struggles
whenever the earlier ones
are betrayed—
"whose spirit is this?"
someone would ask
and not knowing
the outer voice of sky and cloud
think its art makes
nothing happen—
but that *is* something
wandering minstrel of ghostly towns—
see—you made *nothing* happen
not even an abyss
and that has made
all the difference

3.

It's the magic
of perspective
Frank Stella's protractor
drawing the arcs
of round Arabian cities
no bombs or burkas console
no clichés elevate
this debate between
poetry and politics
lifts into theatrical distances
bronze shadows
an archipelago of the embattled
fiddling with their verses
while empires happily burn—
and if all efforts
to render politics aesthetic
culminate in war
I'll be damned if I don't
fire the first shot
or at least see if the reverse
is true and render
my aesthetics political—
temporary overlaps
where archipelagos
bump into one another
in a history of currents and bridges

4.

Tell me
Theodor Adorno
if you know—
is art a logic
that makes reason ridiculous?
Or if it isn't
tell me why the singing ended
when the song wasn't even begun
tilting in the air
at wintering windmills
unfixed emblazoned zones
and fiery poles—
are these means really inappropriate
to our appropriated ends?
You would rather
the language of the pamphlet
when we take to
our inflamed Internet sites
thinking politics lacked poetry
when it was poetry
lost its politics
and set off for a world
of *its* own—those
archipelagos again—
dear everything
I could ever imagine
addressing—
I think there's still a place
call it a compression zone—
the art of activism
the activism of art—
where words are

flagrant portals
dimly starred with
the voices of others
and ourselves
pulling islands across
ghostly demarcations
listening to the keener sounds
of our yet close breathing

Almost Islands

1.

People of earth
I have been to a
small place its
farms paved under
spiderweb freeways
its waterfront ported
for international flows
free-trade zones
of temporary exploitation
all the seeds
we'd thrown there
and the wind
and the people there
so fluid hurtling
in steel over bands
and through tubes
criss-crossing monocultures
they could not for
a moment think of
a future that wouldn't
arrive by container
or slip amongst
the thicket of highways
and overpasses dumped
on drowsy estuary

It's not that
nothing roots here—
place of hawks
and herons the
seeds of windblown
species on the
outer arc of
land forms—it's
time pushed the spit
out at the end of
a river and gathered
a rogue island from
its gulf of orcas
and feathers and
anchored it with a
strip beings could
escape south on and
imagine they were
gone or almost absent
at night in their
split-level homes

It's difficult to
imagine once-buried
tips of mountains
interspersed with
now extinct species
places transformed
Boca Kwomais
Isla de Zepeda now
Punta de Zepada
or better Tsl'elup
I want from now
everlasting and
Chelhtenem (Lily Point)
centre from which
underground passages
radiate—caribou elk
salmon spikemoss
bracken dunlin
American wigeon
sweet gale hardhack
Kulshan that *bleeding*
wound memoranda of
hemlock and cedar
fiddlehead tundra swan
white-fronted geese
devil's club charcoal
reef nets for fishing
our temporary together
a knot in cedar holding
this wayward land ashore

People of earth
I'm fond of nebulae
but my eyesight's
going or the
backyard I inhabit
on cool shady evenings
is getting farther from
the sky jets cut across
on their blue paths
or birds of prey
closer yet smaller
are pestered by crows
which are the most
common of all and
probably much smarter

It's here I realize
there's water on most
sides of me and
sometimes I smell
the sea or a hawk drops
a claw or clamshell
in the driveway though
it could be the crows
and it's not always easy
to tell which one is
the invader or which
shipments will poison us
for those distant profits
going over threshold
gene-flow trajectory
of biotic state shift

People of earth
this place is a
template we can
trace as birds move
as ships and trains
follow evolving markets
everything is a transit
of bio-social flows
who came here first
is no question
who came here to
kill who had monetary
eyes genocide teeth
and debt hunger gut
a market at the end of
each colonizing arm
sweeping the dust
from their charts
and waving at
osprey and eagle
that is a question
we can and must ask

I have this suspicion
starfish and death camas
we came here to this
southern promontory
across sedge and
sphagnum of marsh
and bog to get out
from under the clouds
of mountain rains
but the clouds are
plastic forms the sea
is dropsy turf we're
doing molecular work
now seeding atmospheres
of other worlds we'd form
and such weathers as we
unwittingly make follow
us into subdivision their
tools at the ready
chemical rain and
tanker phosphorus
radioactive sea junk
rolling as whale bait
the tides hunting in
the bow about to
throw their harpoon
climates at us sounding

People of earth
there are no islands now
the planet is peninsular
jutting in space
one blue-green growing
brown orb attached to
disease we've made in
threshold song no
isolato on genetic shores

How does the predator
become the trustee?
Musk gesture pheromone
or mode of socio-economic
production—so species
no island for flit
of swallow's blue-green
back rustle of genetics
in the ditch we probably dug

The next revolution
is what culture will teach
we can and can't do
as system's feedback loop
grabbing the red flag
spore poppy claw
of the biotariat
and heading off into
the weeds developers
left back of decay

2.

Threshold song:

no economy is an island

no oil company
no carbon
no footprint
no government
no coal port
no peat bog
no pipeline
no muskeg swamp
no container
no party
no society
no nation
no species

is an island
entire of itself
piece of continents planets
part of the main

If a clod be
if a seabed a
sound opens
if smallpox spread
if villages gone
midden under highway
if promontory wave
at splendour soaked
if a settler escape

to escarpment home
if a season
if midden
if highways on top
we'll be
lower than the tides
and hungry as sails

Threshold song:

If an oil spill come
if a river
if some coastal waters
coil about islets
tanker cringed
it will be done
and any seal's death
diminishes me

any cormorant's
any otter's
any salmon's
any orca's

because I am involved
in all the water world

so never send
to know for which
species science tolls
it tolls for thee
and all and every
this climate
this cove

Shift of
sea sedge
world in and
out of water no
boundary to bay
our economics
no islands no
ecos to home
and if we are back
at the commons
if nothing not
connected to
everything else
if spilt spit and
pander prose
these megaprojects
take all of us
down where the
single imagines
islands of wealth
on bottomless seas
only not insular
but peninsular
we remind no
capitalist no oil
sand under the sea
no liquid natural
gas fracked up
for portfolio home
is an island and
we all don't share
or suffer consequences
the same

What does not change
is the sill of change

Threshold song:

if planetary scale
if Cambrian explosion and
if glacial interglacial
human forcings
over footprint earth
if biotic effects
if forced by present drivers
then shift state to
a forever beyond
now we'll pollute
or protect this world
trustee shift for
threshold song
worn down by water
weeds overtaking
millennia while
somewhere outside
genes and memes
words may echo down
through repetitions
and their sea change
be a passage always
somewhere rich and strange

3.

People of earth
what is a home?
It is relations
ecosystems a
nexus I frequent
in mud flats
my canoe over
eelgrass beds
escarpment facing
the sea midden
found beneath
tides that sound
interpretations
of now and never
when the revolutions
we need after crashing
markets and biome
involve us stepping
back and letting
other beings flourish
where we once overgrew
come planetary revolution
we'll gladly matter less and less

River built place
grassy sea
island rivered to land
what have we done?
Hidden outside hope
pushed south past marsh
into boggy rapture
a pocket of America
in our Canadian pants
fishing around for change
you must change
your social metabolism
all this ported activity
container carved
farms occasional
greenhouse production
as we slip away from
elsewhere while money
is fashioned into
exquisite kitchen fixtures
and change is a matter
of reseeding the lawn
this avalanche green
this pretend prairie
where the only commons
is a park where we try
to hide from the rules
and the bankers amongst us
as ducks from the cameras

People of earth
we will find ourselves
in some suburban
hallway some darkling
place where no pictures
of ourselves hang
and everyone we know
is a grimy extra
in the background of
some more notable
person's portrait
holding their horse
or cutting their lawn

We will pen letters
blank as clouds
a sea will come suddenly
round peninsulas we
thought islands
drowning every dog
after Prometheus has
shaken off sparks we
will burn our dead
fossils to light cities then
burn the cities too

I like any other
aerial or flashing
will be watching this
Google Earth will only
show narrow tapering places
a coat soaked in blood
will be held out for me
to put on a torch readied

to lead the procession
beneath the drowning earth
radiating passages
as some other I
could have been
will be portrayed
leaving by a door sweep
of his richly draped arm
just now reveals in
back of the oil painting
prime ministerial and
good only for greed

No one is an island
but peninsular
we'll carve our
escape routes south
think the garbage
won't heap the
coal not smoke
the chemical not leach
the sulphur of our
engined desires not
poison the clams
we yet dig the crabs
we gather from
ghost pots we offered
disease to in blankets
of capricious death markets
and the smoke of dreams
the tides will carry
round our promontory lives
disquisitous blind
and sharp as legislative
clubs against our heads

People of earth
seen another way
it's almost miraculous
where miraculous
means the potential
for something else
to still occur still
exist still not be
choked out the
other side of this
threshold song this
state shift we'd
shift the state from

So here it is—
suburban barricade
of turf and lawn
clippings cuts the
highway to the port
a housing development
declares it's not
doughnuts and garden
centre goes off in boats
in the sea legions
of fish gather and
drive a wedge between
the dock and the
ship awaiting its
containered dream
salmon pour upstream
arched and red as flags
a herd of caribou
unseen in these parts
for centuries occupies

estuary and ducks
in droves land and
take out the dykes
letting the Fraser
run where it will

And still we are no
islands entire ourselves
no solitary delicate beasts
for whom a threnody
pulls to a halt outside
all rights of animals
recognized and their own
wilderness crowns
as the climate smothers
fossilized mines
in its smoke arms and
all mechanism grinds
down under the species
bodies being thrown
against its levers and gears

Never too near
what was to be spent
made it fungible land
so others could clam
the bay after forests
cleared the shore
its map ten thousand years
ago whole delta under
waves but still we are
anchored our canoe on
the unspent bay
an imaginary spit that holds
a slim midden in the mind
weaving us into spider looms
and the dream passing there
over shoals of the common good

Notes and Acknowledgements

The first principle of The Barricades Project, to which *To the Barricades* belongs, is taken from Robert Duncan: "We begin to see that the intention of the boundless is manifest in the agony and restoration of pages or boundaries or walls" ("The Delirium of Meaning").

A second principle can be found in Walter Benjamin: "This work has to develop to the highest degree the art of citing without quotation marks. Its theory is intimately related to that of montage" (*The Arcades Project*).

If there is a third principle, it may be contained in the following passage from Rancière:

> Suitable political art would ensure, at one and the same time, the production of a double effect: the readability of a political signification and a sensible or perceptual shock caused, conversely, by the uncanny, by that which resists signification. In fact, this ideal effect is always the object of a negotiation between opposites, between the readability of the message that threatens to destroy the sensible form of art and the radical uncanniness that threatens to destroy all political meaning.
>
> (*The Politics of Aesthetics*)

To push through boundaries towards the boundless (which is tangled there)—to mix appropriation of found material with lyric expression to the point that the one becomes indistinguishable from the other—to practise a dialectic of "readable" political signification and uncanny shock—these are the pathways of this poetry. A lyric voice takes up procedures and citations because they are the world in which it finds itself embodied, a co-embodiment of the address "Dear Common" that someone calls out to anyone else there. "Lyric," writes Thom Donovan, "relates the body of the poet to a poetics of collective affects" ("Lyric's

Potential," *Jacket2*). So we try here, in a lyric space in which we must continue building resistance.

This volume is part of an ongoing long poem project that always seeks "plausible deniability" that it is in fact a long poem project. Everything I write is thus part of some inaccessible and inconceivable totality outside the work itself. Part of its fight is thus with itself, and with "culture" as such. The barricade made of language is both boundary and call for "beyondery"—an outside still to be practised. But there's that other boundary looming everywhere here too: how and when do we cross over from word to world, from text to action? Does the poem barricade us from a world of "doing things," postponing action? Does it wall us up in the "merely cultural"? These poems, increasingly, have been written *between* actions in the streets. They hover there— a boundless boundary around the bound. The gaps and spaces between poems and pages and books are inhabited by "activism," by a body amongst bodies in streets. Dear Common. Let's speak our way into action, into each other's arms, into new shared futures, into new speeches at new barricades thrown.

If this is "documentary poetry"—and it is certainly as much researched as it is lived—it is a documentary of social affects, past and present, of collective expressions of desire, of hope, of outrage, of solidarity, of defiance, of the endless call from the commons for "liberty or death." It is a documentary of the spirit of resistance and revolution. The address of the insurgent impulse, to all potential insurgents, to all tomorrow's insurgent parties.

▢

I am not always careful about keeping track of the sources I use in my work, though many of them are strewn throughout my journals. Part of my impulse with The Barricades Project is to gather material quickly, only to spend a long time editing it thereafter. I also enjoy not being able to discern where source ends and "I" takes over. Indeed, I wind up sounding more and more like another as I continue to work my materials. However, I will attempt some recollection here.

The "screens" on pages vii–viii and 111–12 incorporate every reference to "barricades" in Victor Hugo's *Les Misérables*.

"Dear Common: Vancouver Alights" was written in response to two exhibitions at the Vancouver Art Gallery: *Roy Arden* (October 20, 2007–January 20, 2008) and *Mark Lewis: Modern Time* (October 13, 2007–January 6, 2008). Material was also derived from David Harvey's *Spaces of Hope* (Berkeley: University of California Press, 2000), Earle Birney's "Vancouver Lights" and Michael Turner's "Fred and Ethel" in *Fred Herzog: Vancouver Photographs* (Vancouver: Vancouver Art Gallery and Douglas & McIntyre, 2007). A version of a part of this poem was published in *The Capilano Review* 3.14 (Spring 2011) and dedicated to George Stanley.

"Kettle: Vancouver to Toronto" was written in collaboration with Cecily Nicholson, while she participated in the Toronto G20 protests in June 2010. The poem printed here is my half of a call-and-response series, which we issued as the chapbook *Kettle* in 2011. Much thanks to Cecily, her words, her integrity.

"Dear Common: Study for the rue Saint-Maur" responds to Thibault's famous daguerreotype, a surveillance photograph taken on the eve of Cavaignac's June 1848 assault on the Paris barricades, now in the collection of the Musée d'Orsay. I photographed the same street, exactly 160 years later, in June 2008. The "hidden quotation" is from Celan's "Death Fugue."

"La Commune" draws heavily upon a variety of sources, among them Alain Badiou's *The Communist Hypothesis* (New York: Verso, 2010) and Peter Watkins's film *La Commune (Paris, 1871)*. A version of the poem was written in collaboration with Clint Burnham, Mercedes Eng, Ray Hsu, Reg Johanson, Kim Minkus, Rita Wong, and Cecily Nicholson; performed at VIVO Media Arts Centre on May 28, 2011; and published in *West Coast Line* 71 under the title "La Commune—To the Barricades." Thanks to these inspiring poets.

"To the Barricade on rue de Tourtille." Some lines taken from Marx's 1843 letter to Arnold Ruge. A photograph of the cobblestones on this street taken in June 2008 appears on page 31 of this book.

The "Reluminations" poems originate in John Ashbery's translation of Rimbaud's *Illuminations*. They have been transformed by a variety of procedures and encounters with other texts (such as Walter Benjamin's *Illuminations*) — including that very old procedure, "self-expression." The final version was drafted in Canterbury, England, and is dedicated to David Herd and Simon Smith.

The original draft of "Between Symptom and Critique" was written while Rob Budde read and lectured at Simon Fraser University in 2010. Adapted thereafter.

"Come the Revolution" contains lines taken from the Zapatista statement released on December 21, 2012, following peaceful marches throughout Chiapas announcing the movement's resurgence.

"Dear Common: Politics Is Its Own World" takes its title from David Orr's "The Politics of Poetry," posted on the Poetry Foundation's Harriet blog. Material from another Harriet blog post, "Hives," by Martin Earl is also incorporated, as well as material from Gerald Raunig's *Art and Revolution*.

"Almost Islands," aside from the obvious material taken from John Donne's "Meditation XVII," also borrows terms from "Approaching a state shift in Earth's atmosphere" (*Nature* 486, June 2012). The final section includes lines from Phyllis Webb's "Days of the Unicorns." This is the first poem I've been able to write explicitly about the peninsula I have called home for the past ten years: Tsawwassen, which was once an island several kilometres offshore, now gathered in by the delta the Fraser River pushed south of Vancouver. This fertile farmland is currently being swallowed up by expanding container and coal ports. Thanks to the Tsawwassen people, upon whose traditional lands I now live. I read a version of this poem in 2012 during the 100,000 Poets for Change Earthwalk in Vancouver's Stanley Park, which was included in the chapbook *Earthwalk* (Moonwillow Press, 2012). Thanks to Mary Sands Woodbury.

Thanks to the editors of publications in which these poems have previously appeared: *West Coast Line*, *The Capilano Review*, *W2010*, *Poetry Is Dead*, *Armed Cell*, *Peter F. Yacht Club*, *Crodite*, and *The Poetic Front*. Work also appeared on The Future of Occupy website and the Occupy Vancouver media blog. Some poems were previously published in *Lever* (Nomados, 2011) — thanks to Peter and Meredith Quartermain. Thanks also to Amy De'Ath, Thom Donovan, and Rodrigo Toscano.

STEPHEN COLLIS is the author of five books of poetry, including the Dorothy Livesay Poetry Prize–winning *On the Material* (Talonbooks, 2010) and three parts of the ongoing Barricades Project: *Anarchive* (New Star, 2005), *The Commons* (Talonbooks, 2008), and *To the Barricades*. An activist and social critic, Collis's writing on the Occupy movement is collected in *Dispatches from the Occupation: A History of Change* (Talonbooks, 2012).

Collis is also the author of two book-length studies, *Phyllis Webb and the Common Good* (Talonbooks, 2007) and *Through Words of Others: Susan Howe and Anarcho-Scholasticism* (ELS Editions, 2006), as well as the editor, with Graham Lyons, of *Reading Duncan Reading: Robert Duncan and the Poetics of Derivation* (Iowa University Press, 2012). His first novel, *The Red Album*, is forthcoming in 2013 from BookThug.

Collis teaches contemporary poetry and poetics at Simon Fraser University in the Department of English.